Every Atom

Every Atom

poems by

Erin Coughlin Hollowell

borealbooks

Every Atom

Book design by Hannah Moye & Selena Trager

Library of Congress Cataloging-in-Publication Data

Names: Hollowell, Erin Coughlin, 1965–author.
Title: Every atom / Erin Coughlin Hollowell.
Description: Pasadena, California: Red Hen Press, 2018. | Includes bibliographical references and index.
Identifiers: LCCN 2017034741 | ISBN 1597099066 (alk. paper) | eISBN 1597099163
Classification: LCC PS3608.O49423 A6 2018 | DDC 811/.6—dc23
LC record available at https://lccn.loc.gov/2017034741

The National Endowment for the Arts, the Los Angeles County Arts Commission, the Ahmanson Foundation, the Dwight Stuart Youth Fund, the Max Factor Family Foundation, the Pasadena Tournament of Roses Foundation, the Pasadena Arts & Culture Commission and the City of Pasadena Cultural Affairs Division, the City of Los Angeles Department of Cultural Affairs, the Audrey & Sydney Irmas Charitable Foundation, the Kinder Morgan Foundation, the Allergan Foundation, the Riordan Foundation, and the Amazon Literary Partnership partially support Red Hen Press.

First Edition
Published by Boreal Books
An imprint of Red Hen Press
www.borealbooks.org
www.redhen.org

Acknowledgments

"Not asking the sky to come down to my good will, scattering it freely forever" and "Up there toward the winter sky" were originally published in some form in *Blast Furnace*; "I also say it is good to fall," "Love-root, silk-thread, crotch and vine," and "The living sleep for their time, the dead sleep for their time" were originally published in some form in *Permafrost*; "Backward as well as forward sluing" was originally published in some form in *Prairie Schooner*; "All goes onward and outward, nothing collapses," "The palpable in its place and the impalpable in its place," and "Life wherever moving" were originally published in some form in *Talking River*; "A uniform hieroglyphic," "Continue your annotations, continue your questionings," "A furlong without sympathy," "Those wing'd purposes," "Tender and growing night," and "In vessels that sail, my words sail" were originally published in some form in *Escape Into Life*; "Ascend from the moon" was originally published in some form by *Rust + Moth*.

I'd like to express my gratitude to the Rasmuson Foundation, the Connie Boochever Award, and the Alaska Literary Arts Award. Many of these poems were written and revised in the time that their support gave me. Many thanks as well to the Willapa Bay AiR and the Vermont Studio Center for providing safe havens where the arts are paramount.

Thank you, Peggy Shumaker for your unstinting support and Kate Carroll de Gutes for your kindness always.

Love and thanks to Kathy Coughlin Nardi and Patrick Coughlin, and most of all to Glenn Hollowell.

In memory of my parents
Leonard James Coughlin & Mary Louise Coughlin

Contents

i

ii

iii

iv

Every Atom

i

All goes onward and outward, nothing collapses

My mother asks me to call my father.
Tell him to come and get me. My father
is sitting next to her on the sofa as she says this.
He is the one who handed her the phone.
Who remains when the labels wear away?

The elderly man who tells me not to worry
is no longer her husband. He dons a stranger's face
each morning. The woman who cannot bear
to open her eyes and see the unfamiliar room
has wandered beyond wife, beyond mother.

The snow today sweeps across the landscape,
blotting out the terrain around my house. First
the mountains disappear, then the water,
the trees on the other side of the road,
the road itself. And now, all is white,

a closed space, snow hissing against
the windowpanes. The world we are born into
is not the one that clings to us as we leave.
White. *Remember the crabapple tree that bloomed
in the backyard?* Such extravagance of pale petals.

There's a photograph of my mother and me standing
beneath it. I was thirteen. I plunged toward everything.
She was perfectly still. *Mother, I'm telling the truth.*
There is white. And the pause that surrounds it.
Snow's small blossoming into the night.

Up there toward
the winter sky

Resident of sleepless
3 a.m., the moon
flings itself from behind

a blind mountain.
Bankrupt cottonwoods
remember their small

deaths and rattle
shadow. Winding
the clock of my life

backward, I sort path
from blunder.
Ice beneath everything.

I was an accident,
but I meant no harm.
How easy it is

now to enumerate
the many small
disappointments

that have worn
my clothing. So simple
to discount kindness

like flickers of chipped
starlight traveling.
To never calculate

distance or love.
I thought forever
was broken. Wrong,

again. Snow
from a clear sky,
not memory.

The last scud of day

I brush away the hours
like the smeary skids of eraser
left over from a project that went
from unwell to undone. Words
scrawled over the ghosts of others
and then rubbed away again.
I would like to say there is some-
thing righteous in this struggle, but

wooden spoon
coffee cup
ashes in the woodstove
book dog-eared and splayed
carrots
bottle cap
cutting board
mail beside the placemat.

I watch through the window
hand stilled, those wild tides
and invasions
and angels
asking questions.
Those clouds
skimming south
on some high hard wind.

Still, the blank page, the blank
page and a memory of my mother
crying behind a locked
door that I can not
set down.

A uniform hieroglyphic

Time isn't thinking of her sitting
beside this man she doesn't know

even though she has slept to the cadence
of his breath for more than seventy years.

Every Sunday her children call
down a long hallway like the braying

of beasts that sounds only slightly
familiar. When she looks in the mirror,

Time has scrawled his mark
over the face she composed. All

those stories piled up as a shield
against people who have shifted, villains

become benign, and then shadows.
Only the small room is left, curtains

drawn, gracious darkness sifting into
every corner, and the world

a uniform hieroglyphic beyond the door.

What have I to do
with lamentation?

Today I am curled
in the smooth cup

of my skull, not
calling, because your

silence may smother
me, may be the one

space too many
after the period.

Mother, look out
the window so

when weather
is the topic,

you have
an answer. No

answer. Let us
pretend I've called

and we spoke
about my hair

or my torn jeans.
Or anything

you used to carry
on about. I still

carry your voice
deep in me, like

a small animal
with sharp teeth

sleeping uneasily.
Let us not

wake it. Let us
be content to be

disconnected.

Night of the few, large stars

Traveling from darkness
into darkness.
Planes and airports like funhouse mirrors

double disassociation:
I slip my skin.
Fetched up here on the shoals of O'Hare,

I wander the chill corridors with other
ghosts, past
shuttered duty-free stores.

Disembodied
voices bell out of boxes
suspended over ranks of empty chairs.

The smear and glitter of the holidays
grits beneath my feet.
Behind me,

the soft snick decay makes laying
down
the cards of my dwindling family:

just ahead,
my hand empty and unstrung.
Sleep is a fading constellation.

Three stars:
                    a king, a shadow queen,
a child who is lost on purpose.

The palpable in its place
and the impalpable in its place

It's not tidy, memory.
A house built straddling a chasm.
The way drifting smoke disappears
against the scraped palette of sky.

Storms moved through our house.
I couldn't see them but felt
the prickle on the back of my neck.
Whispering into all the corners

Do you love me? Do you love me?
My mother standing in the kitchen
doing the dishes, a back that will not
turn. The window blank with light.

And just today while moving firewood,
the scent of dirt in Aunt Stella's garage,
shuff of old Buick, Pennzoil, and damp.
Even in February, my nose remembers.

I could get lost this way, rummaging
through half-fallen barns, prying up
asphalt shingles. Always more to find.
Beloved debris. Careworn ghosts.

With linguists and contenders

I pile up syllables before
I pick up the phone. A bulwark
of blameless word-stones.
The distance between us, miles
and decay. Your anger a quick
fire, tenuously banked.

Do not say *home.* Do
not say *how are you?*
Do not say *I am going*
to the movies. Do not
say *I will see you soon.*
Even *flowers,* not safe.

As a child, I learned curtsy
and smile. I learned not gentle,
not proud. Built high walls
that even now I do not like
to breach. A story trapped
in strata of numb ore.

Do not say *dogs.* Do
not disagree. Do not
say *it is beautiful out-*
side. Not *next month,*
not *on Sunday.* Do not
say *I am sorry.*

Put down the phone.
The ramparts smolder,
small pebbles cascading
from the wreck. What
could words still mean
in such fractured remains?

Waits by the hole in the frozen surface

I remember kneeling before my brother's coffin
        but of my mother's grief there is a hole, as if

I've taken scissors and neatly cut her from the day.
        But not really, because there was my father in a dark

suit with his hand on the shoulder of the hole
        in the front row of the funeral home with its cheap

carpets and the flat gray light that plagues March.
        The wretched scrape of snow. The earth too frozen

to dig a grave, and wind pushing its bitter fingers into
        everything. My sister sat in the same row as the hole

that was my mother, but I sat across the aisle. I had been
        standing for a long time in the back of the room

listening to the little songs of comfort that people
        were offering like mouthfuls of potato salad.

There were bouquets of improbable colors.
        Flowers from far away because nothing blooms

in March in upstate New York except broken green
        beer bottles and soda cans in the dirty ditches.

On the way home, my then husband said that maybe
        it would have been better if my brother had never

been born, and I felt as if I'd swallowed an ember,
        which started burning a hole through the ice,

a hole through the snow, a hole that leaked tears,
        finally, but I don't remember seeing my mother cry,

because some things are not seeable, like your mother
        with a hole in her that you will never be able to fill.

ii

Who learns under it to destroy the teacher

First they taught us how
to put on our white

gloves. How to scrub each
night to keep them clean.

Never mind that I
was six and that boys

just twelve years older
died every day in

the jungle. Rotted
where they fell. We learned

to diaper babies,
to pin away from

the child's skin and
toward our own. How

to curtsy and sit,
ankles crossed, our hands

like sleeping birds in
our laps. Each dinner,

the television
detonated with

gunfire from helicopters.
Mother had me set

the dinner table.
I had been trained which

direction the knife
blade should face. I knew

how to use a shrimp
fork. I could iron

anything smooth. I
was a child, but I

knew that white gloves
and party manners were

best, because when I
was silent, clean, and

neat, my mother
would love me.

Or so I was taught.

Life wherever moving

1.
Imagine your mother
was a turtle. Her great
three-chambered heart

beating between two
hardnesses. Her legacy
a sandy hole or shade

on a riverbank. And you,
left in a leather purse
of an egg. You, a thumb-

nail with yolk, a plod
and scuttle yet-to-be.
A scrap before reckoning.

2.
Imagine your mother
was an oyster. Prior
reveler star-strewing

the ocean with sperm
now releases millions
of eggs that float

in such galaxy.
You adrift, groping
for small moorage,

searching for a lock
your key so fashioned,
nacre not grit.

3.
Imagine your mother
was a cicada. Seventeen
years in darkness

feasting on white root
and the promise of song.
She had to climb,

had to split herself
to gain wings. What
more could she give

you but the chance
to do the same?
Transfigure or perish.

For the fourth-month moon showers have,
and the mica on the side of the rock has

shine, glisten like that sleek lick
of damp left behind by a snail.

Or tumble of spume on sand
as the tide pulls back and considers

its gleam. Or the rim of clean glass.
The way an old dog's eye becomes

a lantern out of the dark yard.
Dime spilled from a pocket. Or

a pearl swaddled in silken flesh
still inside the shell. Let me place

within this compendium the split-
open peach. And the parking-lot

puddle with its wavering rainbow
we always passed by too quickly, when

I was small and the world still full
of that transfigured type of spark.

Continue your annotations, continue your questionings

Then even though we closed our eyes
we could still see how disappointment
had become a church we helped you build.

Then there were all those ways to keep
sacrificing. Over sixty thousand miles
of blood vessels to empty, to pack with ice.

Then we learned to hide. We made a tree-
house of our wish to be birds that did not
eat on the ground beneath the feeder.

Then we forgot. We became nostalgic
for open windows and summer curtains.
Dinners of cottage cheese with canned peaches.

Then we dreamt we had forgiven our-
selves. Car wrecks and divorces. Shiny
bridesmaid dresses. Filched cigarettes.

Then we began to draw maps to outlying
cities. We made friend with wolves and
long-distance truckers. Our hair grew long.

Then there was the hour we just watched
the sun elbow its way across the hospital floor.
Shadows began to finally mean something.

A furlong without sympathy

blood vessels mapping my eyelids

in the afternoon a jewel of a nap

sunlight mapping the blood vessels

if only I carried the route like that

I carry part of the story you carry

no wonder you sleep in the afternoon

you carry the weight of an explorer

past this life you are mapping us back

to cells made by your blood rooted

in your body we splashed into you

the way a road branches beyond

the map the route a surprise until

you reach a grove of sugar maple

dreaming like the way your heart

moves the blood warm as sunlight

no wonder this life has too many hours

for you to remember your blood

you carried us, you vessel, mother.

Not in any dictionary, utterance, symbol

Swallowing cold river stones, one
by one, until they click and slick
together in the hollow of my body.
I think by now I must be thick

with it, this fear, but no, it whittles.
The more I ingest, the more untenanted
I become. Always at 3 a.m., it visits,
needle-toothed and gnawing, as if it missed

me, missed the way I greet it with sick
recognition and make a place at my futile breast.
For I am the child of a damaged child
who has passed along her desolation.

It is an equation without solution,
this endless subtraction. Not a pit. Not
a vacuum. What do you call a vessel
that is broken, and the pieces scattered?

Nor any more heaven or hell than there is now

1.

How the light sluices across
leaves so new they purl and shine.
How two swallows flaunt above

me, carving wedges of blue. How if
I wanted I could climb
the hill and keep walking on paths

animals have made into green.
Walking into silence except for wind
and birdsong.

2.

How Rita, on the other side of the hospital
room curtain, pushes the call button. The alarm
bleats methodically for fifteen minutes. Again. How

two competing televisions layer laundry detergent
commercials and squalling game shows.
How in the corridor, a woman with lank hair

shouts *help me, help me,* while slamming
her wheelchair into the doorframe,
but never entering.

3.

Put away that scale that once balanced
my mother's pain against my imperfection.
Words are failing both of us. Her face

clenches like a blank fist of regret.
She has become a new kind of distance.
How I can never measure fear. How

I can never measure how untouched
I remain. The hill, the call
button, the silence.

If they are not the riddle and the untying of the riddle, they are nothing

We are built for breaking. We know this
and yet still more babies are born
with their soft skulls and hunger.
What word can stop a bullet? Walking

down the wrong street, a woman is in the sudden
embrace of a stranger drunk on luck's spittle.
All of us put our hope in time, as if simple
accretion will make our lives valuable.

For some people, it rains every damn day.
All of those names etched in stone, all
the different ways we shine ourselves
like tiny moons reflecting a broken code.

We scatter. The sea rises and gnaws away
at the territory we mapped so assuredly.
So many stories we thought we would
never forget. A lost saint for every family.

At night, I rest my lips against my lover's throat,
his pulse beneath carries me along in my little boat
of affection and need. Oh this wreckage life,
the breath of a hare dreaming in a hawk's shadow.

Love-root, silk-thread, crotch and vine

for Glenn

Balanced beneath trees shy with darkness.
I stand watch as the spiders dance,

barely visible, marooned in a pool of light
that spills from a window. Questions

have knocked and shuffled inside me
as I smoothed through the tasks of the day,

until now when a blush and breathing hand
rests on me and the mountain ridge alike.

The spiders brush each other and withdraw,
each soft collision a raindrop releasing,

the surface calm once again. This is
no violence, no affection, just a call spiraling

through cells. I want to hear it,
but you are in the living room reading,

the last link in a chain leading all the way
back to my father. Love's unfathomable

root, anchoring me to the earth.

Those wing'd purposes

A flock of birds, all angular silhouettes,
swoop and wheel in the sky beyond
the glass. I am half listening to the sound
of your television thousands of miles away,
waiting for you to respond to my question
about your breakfast, waiting for any response really
that might indicate that you know who I am.

The birds plunge and glide into the line
of alders that gnarl beside a stream cut deep
into the hillside, earth sandy and soft here.
When you say, *you are my favorite*, I laugh,
shaking my head, splaying my hand against
the window to feel the cold air held at bay.

And then you laugh, too. Afterward, I walk
outside, my hair tangling in branches as I peer into
the ditch the stream has dug. There are stones
the size of babies' skulls that the water has dodged
around. The wrist-width rivulet presses deeper still.

This is how time moves, carving through a life,
rearranging and searching for bedrock.
This is how time moves, dozens of small wings
that burst forth together and dwindle, distant
specks that disappear from the eye.

Entering the suburbs of some vast and ruin'd city

The reek of urine and old cracked linoleum
crawls into my nostrils, lodges in my hair.
At night when I'm far from the hospital, I open
the windows to let the air sweep some

rankness out of my body. But when I step off
the elevator, it's there with the construction paper
daffodils and bunnies that some nurse has taped
in the hallway between signs that remind us

to wash our hands. It's lunchtime and I have arrived
just as the tray is delivered. My mother is sleeping.
She is always sleeping now, opening her eyes
only when one of us shakes her arm and shouts

Are you okay? when it is plainly evident that she
is not okay. The food is pre-chewed, mashed
potatoes and something like turkey, though ground
up with some brownish-gray gravy, overcooked green

beans, and like a miracle, bright pineapple chunks.
My father steps out for salt, so I spread a white towel
on my mother's chest and lap. I take the fork and press
into the potatoes, lift it slowly to her mouth. My voice

is cheerful, my voice says *This looks good*, my voice
asks if she wants something to eat. And for answer

she opens her mouth just wide enough for a half
forkful, the rest sliding down her chin. I grab

a paper napkin to wipe it up before my father
comes back, because I don't want him to see what
a disaster the two of us are. How I am once again
unable to give my mother what she needs. Until

I spear a chunk of pineapple and maneuver it
between her lips and she chews, then turns to look
at me for the first time in three days and she says
good and I smile and she closes her eyes again.

iii

Not asking the sky to come down
to my good will, scattering it freely forever

The crow's compass swings wildly.
See him tumble from the sky, a flung rag,
a scrap of darkness plummeting.

I want to own such reckless practice.
To find the taproot of doubt and dig it out,
be scraped clean on the sun-bleached soil.

Saint Crow, I am a shabby petitioner.
One of your feathers tucked behind my ear,
I am hungry for your sprung song gospel.

Teach me how to scull through the day
with wings pinioned, lucky, afflicted,
ready to abandon this broken and whole.

When I woke this morning, night's trespass
still on the water but horizon igniting,
I pledged myself to your gape-mouthed ministry.

Hurl me beyond the wildfire of my mind
into air. Into that crystalline shatter
so I might, like too-bright light, scatter.

Perpetual payment

If you could unlock the box
within the box within the fist
of meat that beats to its mechanized
meter, you would find my father.

This is what happens when the people
who knew the sinew and thrust of you
have all passed away. What my father
prays for when he opens his eyes

in the morning is probably not white,
or pastel, or even melodic. He has
harnessed himself to each hour, made
a commitment to seeing it through.

Once, he saw a hawk come out
of the woods and snatch a songbird
at the feeder. Once, out hunting
he thought he heard the childlike cry

of a wounded bear. Turns out, it was two
branches rubbing in the wind.
My father's stories built the house
we set on fire and fled from. My father's

stories built a plucky woman on a train
that none of us has ever met. Somewhere
the bear is still bleeding. Somewhere
that mother is still riding the train.

Heap'd stones, elder, mullein and poke-weed

There are edges.

Stone fences half-knocked
and mossy-sided, ruins

All afternoon she drowses
head awry and softly snoring

of playgrounds, rust-riddled
seesaws and untenanted

as the television hoots and bangs
and my father waits

swings, fields snugged
against the ragged woods,

to raise the spoon to her lips,
a towel draped across her chest,

slip-footed streams
running beneath streets,

her memory darkening and rattled,
a smudge in place of our names

gardens gone jagged
flourishing in green confusion.

This is the meal equally set

Not the car crossing the road, back road with no
centerline. Shriek of metal folding and twisting,
even the weeds scorched black and flattened.

Not the darkened bar, the cigarette perched
in the ashtray. Stale haze scumming the mirrors.
The cells gone turncoat, unchecked and malign.

Not the coffee on the edge of the desk, sun-wrung
morning. Then glass shattering, whole office
shattering apart, smoke filling the sudden sky.

Not the weight of white sheets. The click and hiss
of machines doing what a body can no longer do.
A heart panting through a forest looking to lie down.

Not the crawl of time through blood and bone,
the slow unwinding of thought that fragments the day,
until every room has no window, no door to let in the world.

The end will find us all, however it wills. But for me,
open air. Rain or wind breaking into my ready body.
Breath loosened at last like a small wave in clear water.

And now it seems to me
the beautiful uncut hair of graves

From far above we look like clods of dirt
churned up, clods that move around
with stones in our chests, that get on

elevators, that buy each other coffee
and jelly donuts. But on closer inspection,
consider the dance of our hands as we change

the channel on the television or smooth
her sheets. Watch how we try to comfort
each other without words. There is nothing

we can do, really. Our father is keeping
vigil in a straight-backed chair, watching
The Andy Griffith Show while he holds

our mother's hand. The hospital churns
around them. See how I break after
midnight to lie on the ground outside.

The soft pop of worms surfacing.
The muffled screech of siren.
Rain-sodden seminar on transition.

Tender and growing night

All summer, no stars.
Now raspberries wasp-

ridden and overripe.
Brown burrs grasping

in the long grass.
Even the soil too tired

to hold up blossoms
freighted with the first

cold rains. Darkness swells
again, some small surcease.

I want to dream of the way
my skin became a map,

not a destination,
beneath his fingertips.

Dream of the harmless crashes
our bodies flung together.

Back then the night raw,
split open and looping, I thought,

endlessly.

Ascend from the moon

Oh moon, I could breathe you into my body, soft crush
of dark flowers, late hour alchemy of dew-damp soil.
Oh moon, like a rich ripe vowel resting against the roof
of my mouth, utter me into the rush and rinse of the wind.
Late night wind that charges the blood. Blood art.
Blood fuel. Oh moon, moon like a moan, you roll down
my spine, my arms and legs moon-sodden, heavy
with shadow. Be with me like a low organ note,
vibrating in the deep drone of my *oh* body, a counter-
pitch to the brass alarms of each day. Oh moon,
your lantern is lodged in my ribcage, blazing full-bloom.
You pull me by trickle and flood. I lift like a fish
in the moon-inscribed tide. I rise. Oh moon. I rise.

In vessels that sail, my words sail

Consider me washing dishes
after dinner. A bowl, a ladle,
small chime of teaspoons.

Outside, the mountain is the elegant
magician's assistant. Watch as the sun
cuts her in half.

Now she hides behind low clouds that glow.
Now the big reveal. Light and vapor.

If I could shoot
this beauty into your breast like a clean
arrow.

If I could open you up
to the grace and plunge of water
sluicing over a white-and-blue
plate.

Oh Mother, I would
fill you to brimming with this shine,
this satisfaction.

Show you how a strand of spider-silk,
connecting the nothing
in front of me with the nothing

yet to come, sparks as it sails
on the unseen air.

Backward as well as forward sluing

I've been saving little boxes,
empty cans,
jars that held olives or mustard, envelopes,
broken flowerpots, and especially beautiful
bottles
that were dug out of the dump.
Soon I'll begin putting things by:
the goose
that liked to bite your ankles, Aunt Hilda's
Parliament cigarettes,
the crinkling brown
wrappers from a Whitman's Sampler,
a forty-year-old lock of my hair tied with red
ribbon,
the way you say *I love you, too*
when you aren't
sure who I am,
the letters that Dad sent you
during World War II, porcelain angels, and
pictures of us squinting
into sunlight or leaning
on huge old cars in empty parking lots.
I'll tuck little pieces
of years deep
in the drawer where I keep my socks,
just so
when I am alone
at the table,

I can crack open a bottle
and smell the sweet of your cheek
when you kissed me goodnight,
the sheets
clean and smooth, darkness still
an hour away.

There are millions of suns left

So much sun, as if a thrown knife

is vibrating to a stop in the wall just

behind my head but there is no wall

just a buzzing in my eyeballs, an alarm

that makes me sneeze, makes me close

my eyes so that the sky can not

catch me here in the open, even though

I have practiced my whole life to be

this open. So why does it frighten

me? This cold wind that slides between

all my cells like the world's crowbar.

This moment when I understand I will

not go on, that every part of me

will dissipate, even these words,

especially these words will wobble out

and wear away. But right now

I can stand with my eyes closed,

the sun lying to me, saying hush,

you can stay here forever, breathe,

just breathe, just breathe.

The living sleep for their time,
the dead sleep for their time

i.

Your ship has come in. The marketplace spills over with blue
feathers and barrels of honey. There is a man whose skin
smells of cinnamon. A woman whose hair is bound with silk.
Vermillion. You have a secret. It is cruel like a song
can be cruel. Your father buried a trunk of ash or abalone.
Someone offers you a fish whose mouth is filled with berries.
When you say yes, you mean heartbreak. When you say no,
you mean whiskey and rainwater. There is the woman again,
she's waving you toward her. The ground is covered with salt.
Or snow. An owl calls. A clock. The brush of breath follows
the unremembered dream down.

ii.

A fly bangs against a windowpane. It is not night. It is not day.
The wind pushes torn clouds. You are wearing your father's
wool coat. You put your hands in the pockets. Take them out.
There are books on the dusty shelves. They are written in
the language of ash. The ground is frozen. When you say yes,
you mean two branches barely scraping. When you say
no   . You are carrying something heavy.
You have a secret. It smells of sunlight. Silence follows
the unremembered dream down.

iv

Cycles have
ferried my cradle

First day
of school,
the mothers
walked behind
us wearing wind-
breakers and flat
shoes, their arms
crossed.
I don't know
what they
talked about. My
mother walked
a little behind them
and did not
talk. The sidewalk
stretched ahead
of us but I
could feel
them talking,
feel my mother
not talking.
The scratching
twitch of her
silence. Whatever
bound me
to her bucked
under tension
and finally
snapped.

The faster
I walked,
the smaller
she became.

Thirty years
later, she lives
in my throat,
leather-soled
and gray
sky faced.
Cough
and cough,
but I cannot
budge her.
Still the silence
of her folded
arms. This silence
become my own
baffling rage
lodged whole.

Something struggles
to be freed.
Something fierce
and parched
and swelling.

Seasons pursuing each other

Autumn morning ghost moon
like a clichéd currach indeed,
but no less alchemical. Frost
in all the footsteps and hollow

places. A few black flies bumble
against the sun-warmed clapboard
looking for a crevice to spend
the winter. Yes, it's coming.

And for all of us. When
I look in the mirror, straight
back from my temples, paths
of light twist in my hair.

Three cords of hardwood
stacked and seasoned await
their ashes. The cold air tastes
of smoke, that black bitterness

so latched to absence. But not
yet, a few frivolous pansies
still bloom, gaudy and, for now,
invincible.

I also say it is good to fall

Every day, so much effort.
                                        Glass
is neither liquid nor solid. Structure
being the boundary.
                                  A human face
is neither liquid nor solid. A human face
is a culmination of beautiful scars
left
     by a collection of stories. Every
day, I must decide
                                which stories
to believe, which to offer up to the world.

Outside the window, the wind pulls on the trees
silently. Or at least from inside I can
                                                  not
hear whatever the wind is saying, lies
or that simple kind of truth that moves.
Every day,
                    lifting the sky on my back,
pushing down the dirt with my feet,
I am the trees leaning this way
                                            then that.
Or perhaps I am a single leaf, holding
on but turning yellow
                                    with one small spot
of brown.

Depressions and exaltations

It means sacrificing
something soft,
twenty lymph nodes,

for the pliant
fiction that every
day is another door

to open. It means
wishing on birds,
on gravity, on clouds,

on the stone
I carry
in my pocket, stone

the size of an infant's
heart. Far off, a girl
is calling

to her dog,
her laughter spins
like falling leaves.

Wood smoke
twines in my hair
and leather gloves

by the splitting maul.
Even when I forget
calendar pages,

I feel the earth cant.
It means putting away
the porch furniture

and standing
in our dwindling
portion of sun.

Hankering, gross, mystical, nude

Dear Walt,
I see you around town, your scraggly white beard and ragged jacket.
Leaning your bicycle in front of the post office. Camped out in the library,
sleeping beside a pile of books. I can't begin to imagine what your life
means to you, but I want to. Put a sandwich in your pocket. Put soap
in your shower. Put a hat on your rain-wrung head. Age seems
to be shaking its fist at me these days. I've just started to carry
that black backpack of years, and damn if I can bear to put even one
year down. My mother now a ransacked house, every window broken,
and what she once knew she knew is gone. At night, I think of that soft-
focus where faces were hung. And to be honest, Walt, I am afraid.
Fear sharpens my pencil and sends me into the dark to check out
every sound. I am hoping to find you there, hidden in the woods,
your pale knees sunk into the leaf-litter. Oh sure, I know what you'll say,
effusing your flesh in eddies, your mouth stretched open with its habitual
yawp, *hallelujah for these moments churning up the mud, hallelujah*
for the waysides and women and men with their scarred faces,
hallelujah for twigs and flesh. But what about the hornet's nest, just revealed,
hanging like a wad of bad news next to the path where I've walked
all summer? What about this wind which begins to slice us with its shriven
grimace? Maybe it's better to put a sweater on, better to gather blankets
and tea. Hold our lovers close while we can still remember their names.

My voice goes after what my eyes cannot reach

The day will come when
you forget even this:

your breath unbroken
passing in and out

of your body. You will
forget that you loved

the color blue and the way
your husband told you

each morning
you're still the cutest kid in the county.

You will forget to mourn
for everything

you've felt owed and forget
that you like your coffee

light and sweet and very hot.
I will call out to you,

holding my hairbrush,
finally willing to be

still, to not fidget while
you untangle

my hair, your hands running
smoothly over it.

But you will have forgotten
my voice, all

of our voices, whatever
it was we always

wanted from you,
whatever it was

that kept you tied here,
your house

in order, but something important

always gone missing.

Journey work of the stars

In and out
of consciousness,
like the flicker

of a brown bird
wing
in the woods.

My mother
has sunk
and rallied

so often
that my father says to wait—
your sister is coming

tomorrow.
A continent away,
I try to hear

the clock in his voice.
I go
walking to the mud,

tide out
and herons in.
Their whiteness

a type of shadow
in the dusk.
I cannot gather enough

breath.
I open my mouth
to let the night

wind in. I whoop,
pull air, more,
breathing for both.

Her, with my father
standing a shattered kind
of vigil.

Me, with those needles
of cold light ricocheting
in my lungs.

Soft doctrine

The mother builds the house that becomes the body.
A body that can both cringe and boast. I used to look
in the mirror and imagine her face crouching behind mine.

The mother builds the house that becomes her body.
Over the phone I can almost pretend we are following
that same worn script. Then I remember her house has changed.

My mother builds the house that becomes her body.
Her refusal of the world has translated to pitch and yaw,
the ground unreliable and any distance too far.

The body was once the house of the mother. But now
it is a reminder of erosion and fault lines.
She goes where we push her. She dozes all day.

This mother was once the builder of bodies.
Now we gather over the phone lines to discuss
the doctor's notes, the father's weeping.

My body was once a house for my mother. A golden-
haired doll that understood nothing of redemption,
yet knew everything the mother had wanted to be.

My body builds the house that becomes the mother.
The face in my mirror changing, gathering.
The house of this mercy that is both empty and opening.

A grammar of the old cartouches

To make something holy is to breathe it
into the air like the round syllable the owl
repeats into the escaping blue. To make
something holy is to burn it and read
memory into the smoke, let the smoke
inhabit your clothing, your home. Yes,
to make something holy is to take it
inside you like dark wine, hold it fruiting
in your mouth, and know every word
after that swallow will be scented
with the mystery of the sour soil
where grapes put down their roots.
To make of it a song, and to make of it
the song before the song, the one you
hummed in the womb, *three little fishies*

and the mama fishie too. Song with the beat

of a heart. To make something holy

is to carry it without hesitation like a better

self, a little story that entangles the entire history of your world.

And then farther and farther

Now there is a frame. Inside,
all the time you contained me

in your life from lump of cells
to ghost voice on the telephone.

I can't decide which of us
is now outside the frame.

The line of my jaw is getting soft.
Maybe I only thought you were

the rock I pushed away from,
swimming into faster water. Not

that we didn't know how to damage
each other. We did. All that

bleeding disappointment. Worse,
we couldn't stop keeping track.

You loved the blossoms that sang
from the backyard tree, but not

the hard fruit that dropped later.
Sometimes I ate it, green

and sour just to spite you.
I can't imagine anymore that

we'll understand. One of us
on this side. One of us on the other.

Silent and mournful shining

If there was a store that sold
all the music of mourning, I'd buy
a song for you. It would begin
like an industrial river past pulp mills,
the scrabble and the shouts

of men wearing steel-toed boots.
It would end with one finger
tracing circles around the top
of a crystal goblet, a note rising,
drawing sound out of water

that shudders, shudders and subsides.
The music of mourning is mostly
silence like the famous symphony
in which the conductor moves his baton
but the musicians sit, each instrument

still on their laps. The audience
shifts in their velvet seats
until an impeccably coiffed woman
in the third row begins to weep.
The music of mourning is not

her sob, but the endless one-sided
conversation we are now having,
the one in which I repeat
myself trying to describe
this hush into which you've gone.

Every atom

Seven billion billion billion

With a child's impatience, I banged
against the bathroom door. With a child's
sense of being the sun around which all revolves,
I could not wait as you asked, but rather
threw open the door and pushed my way in.

Seven billion billion billion

And there you were, the age I am now, pulling on your underwear, naked
and still damp from the shower. The scars from my entrance into the world,
and from both brothers, and my sister, creasing your belly. The thatch between
your legs, a dark confusion against the white of your skin.

I rushed from the bathroom, fled down the hall, and out the backdoor. My face,
a flame of embarrassment. My face registering a bewilderment
of shame to have even seen your body which I judged a wreck, a shamble,
so unlike my own, which was still smooth and unscarred. Untested.

Seven billion billion billion

Now I look in the mirror and I am
that woman you were. My hands,
my breasts, the width of my hips.
More. When I look into the dark mirror
of my heart, I find the same choked rage, the same
fear crouching low and baring its teeth.

Seven billion billion billion

Sixty percent of our bodies is water. We are pulled to the moon. We run downhill toward the sea, toward dissolution. Much of the rest is carbon, like ash, a smudged remnant of a wild conflagration.

Seven billion billion billion

Mother, let me finally celebrate you
for every atom belonging to you
as good belongs to me. We were
never so very different. Just two passing
memories of the stars that spawned us
and sent us on our way into the dark.

Biographical Note

Erin Coughlin Hollowell is a poet and writer who lives at the end of the road in Alaska. Prior to landing in Alaska, she lived on both coasts, in big cities and small towns, pursuing many different professions from tapestry weaving to arts administration. In 2013, Boreal Books published her first collection *Pause, Traveler.* She has been awarded a Rasmuson Foundation Fellowship, a Connie Boochever Award, and an Alaska Literary Award. Her work has been most recently published in *Prairie Schooner, Alaska Quarterly Review, Sugar House Review,* and was a finalist for the 49th Parallel Contest for the *Bellingham Review.*